Table of Contents

A Baby Hippo!

Look at the
baby hippo.
Hello, calf!

4

Too Cute!

Baby Hippos

by Rachael Barnes

BLASTOFF!
Beginners

BELLWETHER MEDIA
MINNEAPOLIS, MN

Blastoff! Beginners are developed by literacy experts and educators to meet the needs of early readers. These engaging informational texts support young children as they begin reading about their world. Through simple language and high frequency words paired with crisp, colorful photos, Blastoff! Beginners launch young readers into the universe of independent reading.

Blastoff! Universe

Reading Level

Grade K

Grades 1-3

Grade 4

Sight Words in This Book 🔍

a	find	may	water
and	get	on	
at	her	play	
big	in	the	
by	look	they	
eat	make	to	

This edition first published in 2023 by Bellwether Media, Inc.

No part of this publication may be reproduced in whole or in part without written permission of the publisher. For information regarding permission, write to Bellwether Media, Inc., Attention: Permissions Department, 6012 Blue Circle Drive, Minnetonka, MN 55343.

Library of Congress Cataloging-in-Publication Data
Names: Barnes, Rachael, author.
Title: Baby hippos / by Rachael Barnes.
Description: Minneapolis, MN : Bellwether Media, Inc., 2023. | Series: Blastoff! beginners: Too cute! | Includes bibliographical references and index. | Audience: Ages 4-7 | Audience: Grades K-1
Identifiers: LCCN 2022036377 (print) | LCCN 2022036378 (ebook) | ISBN 9798886871098 (library binding) | ISBN 9798886871975 (paperback) | ISBN 9798886872354 (ebook)
Subjects: LCSH: Hippopotamidae--Infancy--Juvenile literature.
Classification: LCC QL737.U57 B37 2023 (print) | LCC QL737.U57 (ebook) | DDC 599.63/51392--dc23/eng/20220729
LC record available at https://lccn.loc.gov/2022036377
LC ebook record available at https://lccn.loc.gov/2022036378

Editor: Betsy Rathburn   Designer: Jeffrey Kollock

Printed in the United States of America, North Mankato, MN.

Life in the Water

Calves live by water. They live in big **herds**.

herd

Calves cannot swim! They walk underwater.

They stay
close to mom.
They drink
her milk.

drinking
milk

mom

Calves may need a rest. They ride on mom's back!

They learn
to find food.
They eat grass.

They play
hide-and-seek.
They learn
to fight!

Growing Up!

Calves grow
big **tusks**.
They **charge**
and bite!

tusk

Calves get huge.
They make a
big splash!

Baby Hippo Facts

Hippo Life Stages

calf   adult

A Day in the Life

drink mom's milk   ride on mom's back   learn to fight

Glossary

charge

to run at something or someone

herds

groups of hippos

tusks

large teeth at the front of a hippo's mouth

To Learn More

ON THE WEB

FACTSURFER

Factsurfer.com gives you a safe, fun way to find more information.

1. Go to www.factsurfer.com.

2. Enter "baby hippos" into the search box and click 🔍.

3. Select your book cover to see a list of related content.

Index